Marketing for Volunteer Managers:

Mastering Its Magic in a New Millennium

Sue Vineyard

1400 I Street, NW
Washington, DC 20005
www.PointsofLight.org

Other books by Sue Vineyard:

Beyond Banquets, Plaques, and Pins: Creative Ways to Recognize Volunteers
Secrets of Motivation: How to GET and KEEP Volunteers and Paid Staff
*Marketing Magic for Volunteer Programs**
*Finding Your Way Through the Maze of Volunteer Management**
101 Ideas for Volunteer Programs (with Steve McCurley)
101 MORE Ideas for Volunteer Programs (with Steve McCurley)
101 Tips for Volunteer Recruitment (with Steve McCurley)
101 Ways to Raise Resources (with Steve McCurley)
Fundraising for Hospices & Other Community Groups (with Judi Lund)*
Secrets of Leadership (with Rick Lynch)
Megatrends & Volunteerism: Mapping the Future of Volunteer Programs
The Great Trainer's Guide: How to Train Anyone to do Anything!
How to Take Care of You, So You can Take Care of Others
Managing Volunteer Diversity (with Steve McCurley)
*Resource Directory for Volunteer Programs**
Evaluating Volunteer Programs & Events
Best Practices in Employee Volunteer Programs
Measuring UP! Assessment Tools for Volunteer Programs (with Steve McCurley)
Handling Problem Volunteers (with Steve McCurley)
*out of print

ISBN 1-58534-031-6

© 1999 The Points of Light Foundation

All rights reserved. No part of this work may be reproduced or used in any form without the express written permission of The Points of Light Foundation. Worksheets may be reproduced for use by the purchaser of the book.

Published by:

The Points of Light Foundation
1400 I Street, NW
Washington, DC 20005
(202) 729-8000
© 1999

For the complete Volunteer Marketplace catalog, call 1-800-272-8306.

Contents

Marketing for Volunteer Managers: Mastering Its Magic in a New Millennium 1

    The Basics of Marketing 2

    What Makes Up Marketing? 4

    Marketing Components: The Five "P's" 8

The Process of Marketing 17

    Marketing Magic in Four Steps 17

    Trends/Data 23

    The Resource Inventory File 27

The Art of Asking 45

    Hidden Questions 46

    Asking Techniques 47

    Motivation and Asking 54

    Diagnosing Objections 56

    Promotional Options 60

Chapter 1

Marketing for Volunteer Managers: Mastering Its Magic in a New Millennium

For most of the 20th century, marketing was not considered an appropriate tool for volunteer programs because it was seen by many to be too "corporate" and "brash" as well as leaning a bit too much toward "hucksterism."

As early as 1973, however, marketing experts who had spent all of their professional lives working with the private sector began to sound the trumpet for a different perspective:

"Many managers of nonprofit organizations have failed to recognize that marketing is as intrinsic to the nonprofit sector as it is to the business community," stated Benson P. Shapiro in an article for the Harvard Business Review in September of 1973.

Unfortunately, for the majority of volunteer managers, marketing continued to conjure up images of con men, arm-twisting, and hype very far afield from the caring, honest posture that volunteer program managers wanted to convey to the public.

Such beliefs resulted in many volunteer administrators having to scramble to add marketing skills to their portfolios well beyond their real need to tap into its magic. They then had to confront older ill-conceived definitions of what marketing is and is not.

By the dawn of the new millennium, all such negative perspectives had disappeared as marketing became a commonly used tool that assisted volunteer program leaders in their pursuit of excellence and effectiveness.

> *"Many managers of nonprofit organizations have failed to recognize that marketing is as intrinsic to the nonprofit sector as it is to the business community."*
>
> —*Benson P. Shapiro*

> *Marketing is the CARING Trade of Value for Value.*

This book is designed to draw together basic information on marketing and present it in a simple, useful format that you as a volunteer program manager can put to use immediately. The bibliography at the end will help you explore greater depths on the topic and expand your knowledge base regarding the magic of marketing.

THE BASICS OF MARKETING

Let's begin with the most fundamental understanding of what marketing is, as accepted by public and private sectors:

MARKETING is the Trade of Value for Value.

Let us then add one word that seems to make this definition even more acceptable in the third or voluntary sector of our society:

Marketing is the CARING Trade of Value for Value.

The addition of this single, powerful, and descriptive word, "caring," seems to soften the definition of marketing and convert it into language that is acceptable to those who lead volunteer efforts.

Without this added word and the message it conveys, marketing would run the risk of being viewed as a hard-sell, arm-twisting, manipulative tool used to entrap people through guilt trips and false promises.

With the word "caring" added to its definition, however, the true magic of marketing shines through as it sends the message, "When we establish a relationship with others, it will be based as much on what those others get from this relationship as it will be on what we get in exchange."

This translates into volunteer managers making sure that people are placed very carefully into jobs that match their skills, desires, interests, and capabilities and that allow them to successfully serve targeted clients. The satisfaction they therefore derive in that placement is equal to or even greater than what the program itself realizes in work accomplished.

The "caring" component of the marketing definition means that when we recruit we will avoid those less-than-honest methods of recruitment that are only concerned with filling job slots and ignoring the needs of the volunteer. Sadly, such placements have been around for decades, including:

- *First Warm Body Through the Door Technique:* The volunteer manager is desperate to fill the slot of PR chair at the synagogue. Suzie is dropping off her five-year-old child for playschool on Friday when the volunteer manager corners her and aims straight at her guilt spot: "I need a PR chair to help me; we've been friends for so long, I knew you'd help me out...you've never been one to let a friend down!"

- *Buffalo Bill Method of Recruiting:* In a meeting of the PTA board, no one wants to take on the job of Fun Fair Chairperson. Like the method used in killing a buffalo that depends on one such animal straying away from the rest of the herd, the board elects John, who unwisely had stepped out into the hall to take a cellular phone call! Again, the focus is on the need to fill the position, with little regard for the volunteer being dumped upon.

- *"There's Nothing to It" Ploy:* This recruitment and placement method is based on keeping the truth from recruits in the belief that even after they find out they have taken on a hornets' nest, they will not abdicate their position because they either "don't want to let the program down," or they won't let anyone know they are in over their head. Recruiters paint a rosy picture and withhold information in order to "con" volunteers into accepting a job. Yet again, the goal is to fill the job slot with no regard for how the volunteer will feel in the role.

All of these negative examples of placement, and others you have experienced, are NOT marketing. They are false advertising at its

> *" These negative examples of placement are NOT marketing. They are false advertising at its worst. "*

> *"When marketing efforts are rooted in a CARING trade of value for value with an honest concern that everyone involved will benefit from the exchange, marketing can weave its magic."*

worst, salesmanship at its sleaziest, and result in long-term distrust, dissatisfaction, and disillusion on the part of volunteers.

When you add to this the fact that many volunteers who have been so improperly treated will tell others about their sad experience, you have what is termed "de-marketing." This is "word of mouth" that turns people, including potential supporters, OFF rather than ON to your program!

When marketing efforts in a volunteer program or community service effort are rooted in a CARING trade of value for value with an honest concern that everyone involved will benefit from the exchange, marketing can weave its magic.

What Makes Up Marketing?

After setting the tone for marketing, it is essential to understand the language of marketing, beginning with three basic definitions: Publics, Markets, and Exchange Relationship.

Examples of Publics:

Girl Scouts, senior citizens, real estate agents, artists, PTAs, the National Guard, St. Paul's Lutheran Church, pet owners, and ex-Marines.

Publics

These are identifiable segments of society, either by name or makeup.

There are literally thousands of publics surrounding any volunteer effort. The yellow pages and phone book of any community offer the start of a list. The Chamber of Commerce has lists of groups that each have subgroups which are also identifiable publics. For example, any church or synagogue is a public, as are the choir, youth groups, members, spouses of members, women's circles, and ministerial staff that are a part of that house of faith. Similar examples of subgroups can be found in schools, businesses, organizations, subdivisions, public offices, government entities, and associations.

There are some categories of publics that are important for volunteer program managers to recognize:

- *Input publics:* Those identifiable entities that provide services, goods, control, or people. They give something critical to success such as supplies, direction, regulations, support, or information.

- *Internal publics:* Those people who are already part of your efforts: volunteers, staff, and clients.

- *Agent publics:* Those people or groups who speak on your behalf: for example, counselors who send you clients, or churches or synagogues who provide you with volunteers.

- *Consuming publics:* Those people or groups who use the services of your program or organization: clients, the general public, and members. Please note that volunteers can exist in all of these categories. No wonder they are our best recruiters, advocates, story-tellers, and community contacts! Use Worksheet A on page 14 to identify your publics.

Publics, therefore, make up the broadest category in marketing because they encompass every kind of category or group that exists. A key concept of marketing, however, is that publics are targeted, so we must find a way to sort through all of the groups and/or individuals to identify which ones have what we need. We can then target these publics, making them our markets.

Markets

Markets refer to any identifiable publics that you feel can supply your need AND to whom you can offer something of value in exchange.

When identifying markets from among the thousands of publics surrounding you, you identify those that have what you need and

Examples of Markets:

A Girl Scout troop may assist your health program with its annual blood pressure screening day.

Retired Marines may serve on a speakers bureau, giving short talks to groups that have retired military personnel in their ranks, to share information on the special services your program offers them.

Intangible rewards

- Feeling good about doing something for others.
- Repaying a perceived indebtedness (to society, a group, or a cause).
- Making a difference.
- Increasing a sense of self-worth.
- Contributing directly to helping others, improving their lives, or increasing the quality of life of someone in need.
- Having fun.
- Learning new information.
- Getting acquainted with like-minded others.
- Filling empty time.
- Putting unused skills or gifts to use.
- Putting faith into practice.
- Setting an example for children, grandchildren, or others.

Tangible rewards for volunteers, donors, and members

- Getting credit at school, work, or in an organization.
- Building a resume.
- Gaining skills to be used in paid work.
- Getting a needed project done that benefits the workers themselves.

Examples of Exchange Relationships:

The Girl Scouts can receive community recognition for their help, credit for a community service or health care badge, experience in meeting the public, and an enjoyable day learning to serve others.

continued

seem the most likely to supply those needs in an equitable exchange relationship.

Your first task is to prioritize potential markets in order of anticipated success in approaching them to ask for their involvement. You then TARGET those most likely to work with you.

Keep in mind that marketing is targeted, not shotgun-style. You want to carefully think out who you wish to approach, what you will ask for, and what you have to offer in return.

Exchange Relationship

An exchange relationship refers to what you can offer a target market in exchange for their involvement.

When we begin to think of what we might offer in exchange for having our own needs met, we tend to think only in tangibles—the Girl Scout is awarded a badge, for example. We have to broaden our thinking to encompass more intangible rewards, as they are often at the core of why people volunteer or invest their resources.

- Reinforcing new behavior by helping others acquire these same behaviors (12 step programs, for example).
- Receiving a stipend, uniforms, job experience, or insurance.
- Earning post-service rewards such as college tuition.
- Getting pins, plaques, and awards.
- Getting letters of reference for future job searches.
- Making contacts that might benefit them socially or at work.
- Getting attention from their boss.
- Gaining public recognition.
- Building credit for future efforts such as political campaigns.
- Building and leaving a legacy.
- Getting acquainted in a new location, company, or neighborhood.
- Fulfilling expectations or requirements in a company, club, or church.
- Fulfilling a sentence imposed by a court.
- Earning a prize or gift by their participation, such as a bike to the walker who brings in the most sponsors in a walkathon.

The above lists in both categories could go on and on. The key to understanding an exchange relationship is that which is offered in return for the volunteer's involvement must be something of value to the volunteer. Exchange relationships are only as solid as the perception by both parties that they are going to receive something of value in their working together:

- The volunteer program gets the help it needs.

- The volunteers who do the work get whatever THEY feel is a valuable reward for their involvement.

In short: REWARDS MUST BE USER-ORIENTED.

If what is offered in return for becoming involved is NOT perceived by the volunteer to be valuable, there will not be a solid exchange relationship. When I was traveling extensively, a group asked me to volunteer for them and believed that what they could offer me as a reward was the fact that I would get to travel at their expense all over the Midwest. That was no reward for me—it would have been a burden!

Those who volunteer to be on a speakers bureau gain the satisfaction of knowing that other retired military will become aware of the benefits available to them in the community. They also have an opportunity to network with comrades throughout their own area.

> *"Exchange relationships are only as solid as the perception by both parties that they are going to receive something of value in their working together."*

Publics, Markets, and Exchange Relationships are the foundation of marketing, and must be firmly understood by volunteer program managers tapping the magic of marketing.

Marketing Components: The Five "P's"

There are five components in marketing effectively.

Very often, when marketing efforts fail in volunteer recruitment, donor acquisition, membership drives, or other efforts, the real culprit is the lack of attention to one of these dimensions:

1. Product
2. Price
3. Production
4. Placement
5. Promotion

Successful efforts typically exhibit a good product being produced at an affordable, fair price, promoted clearly, and accessibly placed for people who are or might be interested in it.

If that sounds a bit like Greek, let me give you a good and then a bad example from real life as to how specific programs have been marketed. Notice the presence of all five P's in each effort:

Example #1

A group of nurses, doctors, and citizens decide to work together to bring a home hospice program to a county near Chicago. The small group of dedicated volunteers does its homework by searching out available resources and programs, looking at models of similar programs, contacting the National Hospice Association for guidance, and identifying key leaders and groups in the medical and health care community that might have the greatest interest in such a hospice.

From the first step in discussing the hospice concept, an overarching vision of the highest quality care and dignified delivery practices is put forth. Quality, quality, and more quality is laid as the cornerstone of every decision and direction. A commitment to wellness of the entire client family is articulated in every communiqué and program description. As work progresses, the measuring stick for success is always the integrity of the service, which each founder understands is the Product of the hospice. This service or Product is continually reviewed for simplicity of use, quality, sensitivity, and effectiveness. Flexibility is built in to facilitate adjustment to unique needs that clients might require. How all of this will be offered and carried out is mapped out to ensure that it will be produced as promised.

This adds up to a top Product to be Produced effectively.

When all their information is gathered, the group begins to approach targeted markets. They offer solid information, are clear about what they want to do, have a realistic timeline for their plans, and share all of this with their prospective supporters. As people and groups "sign on," the founders share their plans with the general public through the media and a speakers bureau whose members tell their story. The volunteers of the founding group also arrange private meetings with power brokers in the county who can make their way easier or more difficult depending on their view of the hospice effort.

As work progresses, the key volunteers keep everyone who has been involved or contacted informed of what is going on, even if they said they could not help. Special attention is given to informing medical staff, religious leaders, and counselors about their progress. They recognize the wisdom behind the old adage: "What I am not UP on I will be DOWN on."

> *"Successful efforts typically exhibit a good product being produced at an affordable, fair price, promoted clearly, and accessibly placed for people who are or might be interested in it."*

> *"What I am not UP on I will be DOWN on."*

> *If you want to launch a major marketing effort, create a task force of professionals in public relations, advertising, or media to help advise you in your planning.*

Plans are made to continually promote the hospice so that donors, volunteers, and client families are aware of services available and opportunities to be supportive. This adds up to good Promotion.

Costs are realistically reviewed—not just the costs in terms of dollars but in terms of time and energy.

The training that is designed for their hospice volunteers includes an examination of the energy drain that such grief and transition can bring. Support systems are designed so that the volunteers and paid staff will understand where they can turn to restock their energies if they experience burnout or excessive emotional stress.

The founders understand that many people who volunteer in hospices do so because someone they loved has been helped by a hospice program. They often feel they have a debt to repay. The founders also recognize that the volunteer director they hire MUST have extensive training in the screening and placement of volunteers. This Director of Volunteer Services will have to be able to know when to accept someone touched by hospice care in their own life and when and how to gently redirect others who would not yet be ready to step back into the world of the dying.

Time commitments and out-of-pocket financial expenses are projected so they can be described to those who might wish to be involved. Plans are created to emphasize the need for extensive training for all volunteers and the strict rules of confidentiality.

All this adds up to an honest appraisal of the costs or Price volunteers will encounter in working with such a hospice program.

Lastly, the Placement factor is examined. The founders think carefully about their county and how and where they will offer services. They give their attention to where they will place their promotional pieces that can reach prospective clients, volunteers, or supporters. They understand that recruitment and fund raising efforts must be placed carefully and work that into their master plan.

They have done it correctly, laying the foundation for success.

And then there's Example #2

Two neighbors share their meaningful experiences in other locations in which loved ones were served by an in-home hospice program. They decide that they will start a similar program in their community. They put an article in the paper on the need for hospice services and how shocked they have been to find that there is no such program available in the area.

They begin to speak at Catholic and Protestant church meetings, as they believe it is a Christian's duty to provide services for the dying. They recruit a retired practical nurse who agrees that such a program is needed. They begin to ask for donations to pay for the expenses of publicizing their drive for a hospice program. They aren't sure about how a hospice program will be run, but they figure that it all will come to them in due time.

They are shocked when they begin to run into resistance from individuals in some of their audiences, including several doctors and hospital administrators who point to the local hospital's hospice services for in-patient and selective out-patient services. Several members of the clergy are critical of their expectation that the Christian community alone should bear the responsibility for establishing and funding this effort. Others are doubtful that the budget the two founders put before groups is realistic. Still others are unhappy that no real answers come forth when questions are asked about how the hospice program will be designed or how it will be operated.

The founders seem to run helter-skelter from speaking engagement to speaking engagement, with little more than panic-mentality and growing frustration at the lack of enthusiasm or real commitments from churches. As time wears on, the two find fewer and fewer groups willing to listen to their pitch and they begin to disagree on how to proceed. Eventually the effort dies a rather angry, agonizing death.

" Make certain that everyone who is to go out in public and speak for your organization is very well trained. Give them more information than they can possibly use! "

> *The 11th Commandment: Thou shall get thy act together!*

They did it all wrong.

They did not observe what I call the 11th Commandment: Thou shall get thy act together!

Well meaning but unequipped to lead such a complex effort, they made classic errors:

- They did not do their homework. The local hospital already had a small hospice program within their four walls and was beginning to offer its services through health extension in patients' homes.

- They only articulated a dream rather than being more specific about a real plan of action. Their enthusiasm, though awesome, was not enough to overcome their naiveté.

- They "lost" people when they could not come up with specific answers on what they planned. Their "product" was a murky, inconsistent vision just off the horizon. They seemed to have no idea as to how to "produce" their hospice vision.

- They forgot to recruit key people from the various publics in their community who would need to be involved, such as doctors, health professionals, referral groups and individuals, or key community leaders.

- They were presumptuous and narrow minded in their admonition to selected segments of the faith community that they had a "duty" to create this hospice. They were also insulting to the non-Christian communities of faith by excluding them in their appeals.

- They totally underestimated the real monetary costs necessary to establish and run a hospice program and antagonized those who tried to point this out by their refusal to listen to experts. They had no answers as to energy or time costs for those who might become involved, thus turning off many who weigh these two factors carefully before "signing on" to any effort.

- There were no real plans for where (or how) the hospice program would be anchored. They seemed to believe that any in-home hospice program would not really need a central location, pointing out again just how little homework they had done BEFORE trying to promote the idea.

- Promotion is a key element of any new effort, but no promotion is better than bad promotion, especially in the start-up phase of planning. These two well-meaning, dedicated, and committed founders promoted a product before it was clearly defined, and had no master plan for telling their story to the public.

What these women did was actually DE-market a very good idea, turning people OFF rather than ON to the idea. Apparently they did not understand the subtle difference between arm-twisting and trying to talk people into saying "yes" to the hospice plan versus trying to remove people's reasons to say "no." (We'll discuss the wisdom behind removing "no"s as we explore the art of asking in Chapter 3.)

Careful attention to Product, Production, Price, Placement, and Promotion are the cornerstones of good marketing efforts.

Publics, Markets, the Exchange Relationship, the Five P's, and a basic belief in the Caring Trade of Value for Value are the critical fundamentals volunteer program managers need to understand marketing and tap its potential magic for the 21st century.

> *"What these women did was actually DE-market a very good idea, turning people OFF rather than ON to the idea."*

Worksheet A
Where Are All Your Publics?

As part of your marketing process to identify what you HAVE, begin to create an information and contact file of the Publics that impact your program. Ask others to continually help to expand this list under the following categories, as shown below:

Input Publics (entities which give something to your program):

Support Publics (volunteers, supportive media, or donors):

Supplier Publics (computer stores, utilities, or national headquarters):

Regulatory Publics (state Health Departments, courts, or national ruling bodies):

Internal Publics Those people who work within your ranks:

   Volunteers:

   Paid Staff:

   Hierarchy:

   Board or Advisory Committees:

   Key Leaders:

Agent Publics: Those who speak on your behalf; advocates.
   Internal: (mentors, key leaders, or other department heads)

   External: (those who send you clients, volunteers, donors, or supporters)

Consuming Publics: Those who use your services or information.
   Clients: (they receive direct services)

   General Public: (those who benefit because of your presence in the community because they are safer, have new information, enjoy what you offer, or see healthier children around their own)

WORKSHEET B
DIFFERENTIATION

This worksheet will help you focus on what makes you different and how these differences can be used in recruiting and fund raising. This is slightly different from "positioning," which is a public perception; "differentiation" is background information to be used to persuade.

1. What does your organization do (the general mission)?

2. What services does the organization offer?

3. What roles do volunteers play in supporting the organization?

4. What other community organizations and volunteer programs serve the same population?

5. How does your volunteer program DIFFER from these others?

6. What similarities exist between your program and theirs?

7. Are there advantages for volunteers in working with you? What are they?

8. What characteristics make your organization and volunteer program unique?

9. How might you capitalize on these unique features?

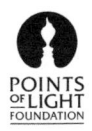

Chapter 2

The Process of Marketing

When first looking at books on marketing, the reader can become overwhelmed at the complexities and intricacies inherent in its many aspects. This may account for the aversion many volunteer managers have in trying to adapt it to recruitment, fund raising, friend raising, and publicity efforts.

In reality, the process of marketing is quite simple, direct, and full of common sense. In my training of thousands of volunteer managers in marketing, a typical comment is, "I've been using marketing skills for years and didn't know it!"

That's correct. Anyone who is organized and does indeed "have their act together" has probably been using the principles of marketing without realizing their own innate competence in this area.

> *A typical comment is, I've been using marketing skills for years and didn't know it!*

MARKETING MAGIC IN FOUR STEPS

The process of marketing is carried out through four steps and in the order given here:

Step 1. What do you HAVE?

Step 2. What do you NEED?

Step 3. WHO HAS what you need?

Step 4. HOW do you GET what you need?

> *Starting with a need first is the root cause of many problems that can follow.*

Step 1. What Do You HAVE?

In teaching these four steps, some people have been convinced that I have the first two steps reversed, believing that we should always first start with needs. The truth is these two are not reversed and starting with a need first is the root cause of many problems that can follow.

Let me share some parallel examples:

- Would you write a check without knowing the balance in your account?

- Would you begin a recipe without making sure all of the ingredients you need are in your pantry?

- Would you jump in your car to begin a long trip without having checked the gas gauge?

For anyone who answered yes to the above, I send my sympathies for overdrawn bank accounts, having to dump half-prepared soufflés, and being stranded in the desert. To the vast majority of you who said "of course not!" to my questions, welcome to the reality of marketing.

Even before you begin to identify needs, it is imperative that you understand all the resources and realities that surround your program, organization, and community. When a need pops up, it can be a very stressful time, which will not be helped by having what I call "resource myopia"—a poor vision of what you might have to trade as a value in exchange for what you might ask from others.

If that "caring trade of value for value" is at the root of your marketing efforts, you will want to know what you can give as clearly as what you can get in a relationship with others.

Focusing on what you HAVE can be an interesting and rewarding exercise, one best accomplished by asking key volunteers, staff, and others connected to you to help identify your assets. Your perspective alone, though all encompassing, is not the same as a client, new volunteer, or seasoned staff member. These people see your program from a different angle, and can therefore shed light on "hidden assets" you alone may not have realized were available.

As you look at what you have, you may also uncover the root source of what you may have dubbed "communication problems" or "volunteer-staff relational problems," as different individuals hold very different definitions of the program's vision, purpose, history, and future. A Meals on Wheels program in Texas discovered why two volunteers were constantly at each other's throats when one defined the Meals On Wheels purpose as "feeding hungry people" and the other saw it as "showing concern through interacting with isolated individuals." Is there any wonder they clashed on how funds should be spent, volunteers trained, and success measured?

As you look at what your program HAS, examine and note the assets or resources in the following categories:

1. Mission*

What business are you in? Ivory soap is in the cleaning business; hospitals are in the wellness business; Amtrak is in the transportation business. The broader the perspective, the greater the chance for success. Hospitals that believed they were only in "the fix-'em-after-they're-broken" business have, over the last decade or so, closed their doors because they were behind the times. Hospitals that recognized the shift in people's thinking from curative to preventative health added fitness centers, screening tests, seminars to educate the public on disease prevention, holistic counseling, nutritional training, and well-baby clinics.

* NOTE: Volunteer managers find themselves in a unique position in that they have two missions they must keep in mind: one for the organization overall (i.e.: offering health care to the community) AND the mission of their program (enabling and integrating volunteer efforts to positively assist in providing patient and hospital service needs).

2. Product

What is your "product?" What do you want people to desire? Remember that people look for products that fill a need they have. Understanding this will help you tap into motivations folks have as mentioned in Chapter One (helping others, repaying debts, or socialization). Your product will also serve your purpose or mission.

It can be very difficult for some people to think of services as products because we tend to think of the latter in more concrete terms, while the former is more elusive. It is critical, however, to distinguish what your product is and how it differs from similar efforts in the community. Funders and others considering support of a program often want to understand exactly what is being offered and how it is different from others in a community. This is called "differentiation" and offers a precise definition of your product and what benefits will be realized if they become involved with you (see Worksheet B on page 15).

3. Positioning

What is your present position in the community? Do people know about you? Are you respected? Trusted? Are you easily accessible? Is your volunteer program perceived as a good place to work? Is it enjoyable? Is it challenging? What exactly is the public perception of your overall organization and your own department?

Be careful with assessment (for example, see Worksheet C on page 42). Gathering people already involved with you will probably not give you a true picture of how the public sees you. Ask volunteers and staff who are active in local clubs, houses of faith, and groups to do an informal survey to uncover how the uninvolved perceive you. Do they know about your volunteer program and clearly understand what volunteers do there? What do they think about your organization as a whole? Don't be shocked at opinions people hold. Even if there is a negative perception or ones that are misinformed, it is valuable information for you (see Worksheet D on page 43 to

> *" Gathering people already involved with you will probably not give you a true picture of how the public sees you. "*

gather this information). You have to know where to start if you plan to enter a race! After getting a clear picture of current public perception as it stands, it is time to begin to define where you want public perception to be in the future. Having a clear picture of where you want to be in the future is critical to good planning. Use Worksheet E on page 44. Racers also have to know where the race route is and the location of its finish line!

In looking at positioning, understand that the best reputation is typically given to the first in anything—not necessarily the best, but always the first. Chrysler minivans are no longer rated the best in America (that distinction goes to Toyota, according to the *Consumer Guide*), yet they out-sell all the other van manufacturers a gazillion to one. Why? Because they were the first and therefore implanted into the consumer's mind as "the" minivan. Think about that when deciding to initiate a new effort. Being first out of the starter block can reap long-term returns. Just ask Lee Iacocca!

> *"The best reputation is typically given to the first in anything—not necessarily the best, but always the first."*

4. Orientation

A "marketing orientation" simply means that marketing is a consideration at every level. Such an attitude or orientation can be seen in the more successful businesses or nonprofits. People from the top down think in terms of marketing—exchanging values, giving a dollar's worth of product or service for a dollar spent by the consumer, telling the story of how the product will benefit a consumer, and adding value.

For a volunteer program to be successful in marketing itself to the public, there needs to be a marketing orientation or appreciation in the minds of anyone who might govern actions: CEO's, department heads, organization leaders, and boards.

Eventually you will have to spend time, money, and resources to market successfully, and you will need those above you who give permission for such expenditures to understand why you are asking for marketing support.

> *Remember that each of us has just so much energy available for our work, and having it drained off by fighting battles for marketing reduces the energies left to do our jobs.*

I have encountered successful volunteer managers who do not have such an agency-wide orientation around them, and thus had to expend considerable energies working around this nonsupport.

Remember that each of us has just so much energy available for our work, and having it drained off by fighting battles for marketing reduces the energies left to do our jobs.

5. *Resources*

After all of the above examinations, which are rather wispy, it may be a relief to move onto more tangible assets you have available that might prompt people to become involved. In the growing trend toward bartering, you will also encounter assets for trade. Those assets might be traded to another organization or group for needs you identify in the future.

Such an example is very prominent in my own home town where a church provides free space and volunteers to an adult day care program for Alzheimer's victims. The church had thought it would have to create its own program when several members encountered the care-giving exhaustion suffered in dealing with this disease. Instead, an established program provided this service and found a home!

With as many other people as possible, brainstorm what you have in the way of assets: equipment, training, a physical site, expertise, contacts, transportation vehicles, experts, sheer numbers of people, information, and location.

At a managerial level, track the monetary assets you have in your budget and projected income.

After all these tangible assets are listed, return to "wispy" by remembering to count reputation, trust, longevity, and positive associations as real assets also.

Trends/Data

Every community around the world has characteristics that are unique to them. Before marketing can truly begin to target specific publics and devise exchange relationships, a program must understand the dynamics that surround them. Your Chamber of Commerce or Mayor's Office may be your richest source of basic data.

You may wish to assign to a volunteer the task of keeping up-to-date on changing demographics of your area, including population numbers and categories by age, marital status, educational level, average income, and income span. A program that wants to begin a recruitment campaign in Boulder County, Colorado and in Dade County, Florida will use different language, approaches, and placements due to the fact that the average age in Boulder is in the mid-twenties, while the average age in Dade is in the high fifties.

The Chamber of Commerce will probably have a list of community agencies and organizations. It is critical to have an up-to-date list of such groups and their leaders, at all times, for possible interaction and coordination. A master calendar should be one of the tools you have as you plan events and campaigns. Take into account the events and campaigns of other groups in town as well as school, religious, and holiday calendars unique to your area.

In addition to the demographics, calendars, and data that surround you, you will need to be in tune with general trends that impact your potential targeted markets. Faith Popcorn (yes, that is really her name!) creates the Popcorn Report on a regular basis, which tracks the major trends found in America that may impact your local programs.

One look at volunteer programs today reflects the trends she spotted for the 1990's, and each year she adds more. In my book *Megatrends*

> *" Before marketing can truly begin to target specific publics and devise exchange relationships, a program must understand the dynamics that surround them. "*

& Volunteerism you'll find a translation of the major trend-watchers into the language and application for our field. Between these two references and updates that are published regularly, you will be able to identify the factors that are helping to shape your program and impact its marketing efforts.

Key among these trends are:

1. Cocooning

People staying close to home, wanting to be safe, surrounding themselves with comfort, having their friends and family close at hand.

Translation

Potential volunteers respond well to opportunities to help neighborhood and community efforts that improve their own environment, making it safer or more comfortable. Opportunities to volunteer as a family unit are appealing.

2. Time

Time is the new currency in America. People are spending more time working, commuting, and fulfilling their obligations than ever before. They make judgments based on how much time things will take, or how they might do more than one thing at once, thus "saving" time.

Translation

Potential volunteers want what I call "hit and run" volunteer opportunities, or episodic assignments that do not require large blocks of time or long periods of commitment.

- They love jobs that allow them to be with family or friends, so that socialization can go on while the work is being done.

> " *Opportunities to volunteer as a family unit are appealing.* "

> " *Time is the new currency in America.... Potential volunteers want what I call 'hit and run' volunteer opportunities.* "

- Parents tell us that they appreciate volunteer assignments that allow them to participate alongside their children, as it gives them a chance to demonstrate helping rather than just talking about it.

- It also, of course, allows them to have more time with their children—a gift they value highly.

Volunteers also respond well to jobs that allow them to take the work home or do it at the office in "down times," thus being able to tuck work into times most convenient to their schedule. The entire issue of time efficiency also applies to energy efficiency—being able to conserve and use energy efficiently with the highest level of effectiveness.

3. Safety

Americans are very concerned about safety. They want a physically safe environment in which to live, learn, and work. Appeals to them to make any of these areas safe are usually regarded as "worth the effort." They want to make sure that affiliation with any group will keep their reputation safe and unblemished. They regard a "no-hassle" environment as one that is safe from stress, and therefore tend to try out any new program at a minimal level to witness for themselves its climate, effectiveness, and integrity.

Translation

Volunteer program managers first need to ensure integrity in their systems, so that when new volunteers "try them out," they will like what they see and sign on for other assignments.

- The physical site must be as safe as possible.

- A risk management audit should be done regularly to ensure that volunteers and staff are not put in harm's way.

> *"They regard a 'no-hassle' environment as one that is safe from stress, and therefore tend to try out any new program at a minimal level to witness for themselves its climate, effectiveness, and integrity."*

- In medical settings, risk management will entail more work and training than in other settings, but all organizations or programs need to be careful about safety.

- Training becomes a valuable tool in establishing the safety of volunteers and staff. Orientations need to be scripted carefully to ensure new people understand safety issues. Volunteers are fully trained to respond appropriately should a crisis arise.

- Trainers are free to ask questions that might dispel any concerns they have in working with you.

4. Relationships

As our world becomes more technologically advanced, there is that old physics rule that comes into play: opposite forces applying equal pressure. The opposite of technology is relationships with living, breathing souls (pets included!). As we find ways to communicate more with others, we are afforded the paradox of being able to AVOID human contact. How many of us have left messages on answering machines, after hours, to avoid having to have a more time-consuming conversation with a rather wordy colleague? How easy is it to send a quick e-mail to someone rather than picking up the phone or seeing them in person? The latest statistics on reasons for divorce puts "time at the computer" as a major factor—rather than arguments about money or child-rearing, which had traditionally topped the list!

Translation

Volunteer opportunities that allow people to be with others, meet new people who share an interest, or work with friends or their family unit are appealing to folks.

- Corporations have found that their volunteer community service efforts are most successful when they allow employees to work together on a project or even involve their families.

> *" As we find ways to communicate more with others, we are afforded the paradox of being able to AVOID human contact. "*

- People who are already starved for time and energy want to work on something that directly affects them, and are also looking for ways to forge new or strengthen old ties with others.

- Working in teams or task forces helps provide volunteers with something of value beyond the simple "feeling good about doing good" sense they get from the work itself.

- In tracking the motivations of why people volunteered, the Gallup Poll on Giving and Volunteering published by Independent Sector in Washington, D.C. and other such studies show several relationally based reasons for volunteering, such as wanting to meet others with like values, wanting to meet people with similar interests, or wanting to get acquainted with like-minded people in their new community.

There are many other trends floating around your program locally, regionally, or globally. It is critical for you to understand what they are and interpret their impact on what you do and what you plan.

The Resource Inventory File

There is an exercise that I have used with every audience I've trained in marketing. It is valuable because it creates a tangible, real record of the resources that surround a program.

First, a Publics Chart for the organization is created—a "map" of the publics that exist. Step Two is the transferring of the information continually gathered or added to the chart into a Resource Inventory File that can be used through the years. It is so critical that I would like to lead you through the exercise here.

More than any other single tool you create and use, this file is the most important. It is your "bank account" that holds the resources you need through the years.

> *More than any other single tool you create and use, the Resource Inventory File is the most important. It is your 'bank account' that holds the resources you need through the years.*

Resource Inventory File Sample

Name: Gloria Dei Lutheran Church.
Grant & Main St., Downers Grove, IL 60515
Established: 1948   Phone: 630-555-1212
Pastors: Gary Heeden, Sue Smith, John Jones

Our Contact:	Date:	Phone#	Affiliation/Position?
1. Sue Vineyard	4/98	555-1234	member; on Christ. Ed. comm.
2. Elaine Adams	5/99	555-2345	member; on Church Council
3. Chuck Enge	2/99	555-3455	member; teacher; Christ. Ed. Chair
4. Rich Daniels	6/01	555-0987	wife is active member; helps on grounds

Misc. information:
1. Church Council meets 1st Monday of every month; if holiday, 1st Tuesday. Full control.
2. Sub-groups: 10 committees: Education, Property, Evangelism, Outreach, Staffing, Membership, Church School, Care & Counseling, Suppers, Events.
3. Member: Evangelical Lutheran Church of America (ELCA).
4. Member groups: 8 ladies circles; singles', seniors', women's, and men's groups.
5. 50th anniversary celebration: Oct. 1998. Char Christ & John Anderson, co-chairs.

The Publics Chart

Gather a group of key volunteers, staff, and even some clients if that is practical for your program. Provide large sheets of paper (flip chart newsprint is great) and give everyone a marker.

1. In small groups of four or five, instruct people to think of all the identifiable segments in their area (these are the publics we spoke of in Chapter One) either by name—"Gloria Dei Lutheran Church" (see sample on this page)—or category—"real estate agents" or "seniors' organizations."

Point out to them that within every public they think of there are smaller publics or groups that make up the whole. Thus, under Gloria Dei there would be staff, pastors, choirs, Sunday school teachers, the governing board, committees, and members. Under senior organizations would be AARP, Retired Teachers Association, and senior park district programs.

2. The next step is the key to a good resource file: Gather all the charts, ask people to look them over, add any other groups or subgroups they can think of, AND ADD THEIR NAME, THE DAY'S DATE, THEIR PHONE NUMBER, and their connection beside any group to which they belong or have direct ties!

All of this information then gets transferred, possibly by a few homebound volunteers or students trying to earn credit in a computer course, into a permanent file that shows groups by name and critical information. What you will end up with will look something like the sample Resource Inventory File sample on page 28.

Step 1 is indeed: What Do You HAVE?

The object of all this is to create a file that not only tells you what groups exist and how to contact them, but offers a list of names of contacts that are connected to you (remember, that's how their name got on your publics chart) and who are already INSIDE that public. In establishing a relationship with any group, it is easiest when you are working with someone already a part of that group. They can guide you in your approach, mapping out a solid exchange relationship, knowing who to speak to first, what might be of value to the group or leadership, how decisions are made, and the best timing for a contact.

All of the homework for this first step in marketing may seem overwhelming, but making sure that you know what resources you can tap, what information sits in the background around any effort you might attempt, and what impacts the ultimate success of any project even BEFORE you have identified specific needs is critical to effectiveness.

When needs arise, especially if they pop up most unexpectedly and demand a quick response, it is much easier to have created a resource file ahead of time so that you can quickly consult it to identify those resources and contacts you need.

> *In establishing a relationship with any group, it is easiest when you are working with someone already a part of that group.*

> *"Not having gathered such background information typically leads to 'resource myopia' and subsequent knee-jerk reactions that often cost time, energy, and money in the long run."*

Not having gathered such background information typically leads to "resource myopia" and subsequent knee-jerk reactions that often cost time, energy, and money in the long run. For example, if you identify a need for printing a two-color brochure, without such a resource inventory you will probably simply hire a printer. With a resource file, you may get the same work done by a high school print shop in which a key staff person's son is trying to earn extra credit, a church with such printing capability that has as one very active member, your best volunteer, or a local utility company looking for some good press for a change!

Step 2. What Do You NEED?

When assessing what your needs are, it is critical to differentiate between wants and needs, as they are usually quite different.

Volunteer Directors would, of course, love a large pool of volunteers able to do a multitude of jobs effectively whenever they are needed. The reality is not quite that simple, however, and therefore we have to identify specifically what is needed: six volunteers to work in the office five hours a week and 12 to work in the mail room twice a month, for example.

Wants and needs are easy to distinguish: A want is a desire, usually pointing to a "wouldn't it be great if..." objective. A need is a "must have to survive or get the work done" objective. The former is the frosting, the latter is the cake.

Having this differentiation in the back of your mind, you can then group needs into categories:

- PEOPLE: Who will you need? In what numbers? For what time periods? When? Be as specific as you can, then separate your answers into categories of long-term commitments and episodic commitments. If you are not sure of the time a job will take, mark it unknown and when recruiting and placing volunteers be up-front on this aspect of the job. Use a master marketing calendar that indicates when numbers of volunteers are needed. This will guide you in pre-event planning by indicating when recruitment will need to begin. It takes longer to recruit, interview, and place high level jobs, with a longer commitment of time than one-day, occasional jobs.

- GOODS: What "stuff" do you need? Computers? Office equipment? Transportation vehicles? Do you need things permanently or temporarily?

- SKILLS: What specific skills will you need to meet your goals and do your assigned work? Computer, graphics, organizational, child-care, or accounting?

- DOLLARS: What dollars will you need? Look carefully at potential bartering with others, so that you might cut down in actual dollars and still meet needs. As resources shrink and administrators demand "belt-tightening," be prepared with alternative ways to meet needs that reduce dollar outlays to a minimum yet still allow you to get what you need. Think in terms of long-range projections.

- SYSTEMS: The climate of an organization is often measured by the satisfaction that workers—both paid and volunteer—sense. Much of this satisfaction comes not just from nice people, but from systems that facilitate work and remove obstacles that hinder success and satisfaction.

As you look at the needs your program has, examine carefully the systems people must deal with as they work together. Are they simple and easy to use? Do they advance the work toward the ultimate goals and mission? Are they focused, avoiding unnecessary activity or busy work? Do multiple systems blend rather than conflict in getting the work done? Do they make sense?

If a careful examination reveals systems that are out of date, unnecessary, ridiculously complex, or frustrating, it is worth your

Categories of Needs

- People
- Goods
- Skills
- Dollars
- Systems
- Support
- Organization
- Services

time and energy to get them into working order. Doing so eases your marketing efforts as well as the other managerial tasks. No recruitment campaign (another phrase for marketing efforts) can reach its potential of success if it is encumbered by silly systems that drain energies, wear out recruiters, and turn off potential recruits.

- SUPPORT: As you plan any effort, identify the support you need, especially in terms of people who can go to bat for you. Your effort to get them in your corner is actually just another type of marketing: You will ask for their support and offer them something they value in return. Often this is simply seeing a shared dream come to fruition, or a success in which they can feel a part.

Strategize what support you need: Public? Hierarchy? Key Volunteers? Key staff? Legal? Organizational? Know ahead of time what you need and make plans to obtain it.

- ORGANIZATION: Who and what within your organization will be needed for you to accomplish your objectives? Identify needs such as dollars, extra staff, specific expertise, supplies, and equipment, and move to obtain them.

- SERVICES: What services will you need to accomplish your goals? Internal, external, or community-wide? Look at the list you made of goods needed and determine whether, for example, you need to obtain vehicles or transportation; a church bus that sits unused all week, insured and fitted for the disabled, may be exactly what you need for a new program for adult day-care for Alzheimer's patients.

There is one more "need" that you and those around you have that is rather elusive, but critical to success. I'll call it a "Marketing Attitude."

By this I mean that you and key people around you are constantly thinking in terms of marketing, looking for opportunities to tell your story, pleading your case, attracting supporters, engaging work-

> *"There is one more "need" that you and those around you have that is rather elusive, but critical to success. I'll call it a 'Marketing Attitude.'"*

ers, setting a vision in the minds of others, finding values to exchange, and developing solid relationships. Everything you do is marketing. It is a constant.

It will limit your effectiveness if marketing is only seen as a function that is stuck in one corner of your plan of action. Marketing, to reach its full potential, needs to be an integral part of all your efforts. It must reach beyond simply being a science and also become a spirited consideration in all activities.

Consider the opportunities to bring marketing into all that you do:

- *Do you sponsor community-wide activities such as a health fair, a site open house, a fund raising event?* Create publicity for each event to include information on how to volunteer for your agency. You are marketing for recruitment.

- *Are you part of the staff orientation in your organization?* Tuck in some well-chosen words on the value of volunteers and how staff can look to you as an internal consultant, ready to help them integrate, supervise, and work successfully with volunteers assigned them (marketing for internal support).

- *Are you invited to speak to clubs, churches and organizations?* Plug specific ways they as a group can help serve your clients (marketing for specific needs).

- *Does your parent organization plan a full page spread in the local paper or a booklet or annual report to the community?* Lobby to have a feature included on the volunteer program and prominently displayed contact information for those readers that might be interested in involvement (marketing for recruitment, support and public awareness).

When volunteer managers, volunteers, and staff all get into the habit of watching for opportunities to piggyback on other efforts to get the word out, marketing will become a part of all aspects of the organization, rather than being relegated to separate campaigns.

> *"Marketing must reach beyond simply being a science and also become a spirited consideration in all activities."*

What you NEED in and for your volunteer program requires careful consideration and targeted objectives, so that you can move easily into the next step in the marketing process: determining who might provide these identified needs.

Step 3. WHO HAS What You Need?

The next step, after determining what you need, is very logical: You must now think about who might have what you need.

This is where you will begin to see the incredible value of your resource file of publics that surround you.

The best way to demonstrate how this third step is mastered is to offer an example:

Let us say that your volunteer program has identified a need for a brochure that can tell the story of what you do, who you serve, and how folks might become involved as volunteers. It is a marketing piece for the purpose of recruiting both people and support. You need it to be three colors, tri-folded, and available in three months. You will need 10,000 copies.

As you check your publics file or chart, you are careful not to rule out any one person or entity in this first scanning of identifiable segments in your community. Saying "no" for someone else can be a dangerous thing and may keep you from establishing a strong relationship that could be helpful to everyone involved. Think of this first step as "need-brainstorming" as you look over the list of publics who could provide your need.

Among your publics you recognize that the following could print the brochures in the quality and quantity you need:

- Three print shops in town.

- The local newspaper.

> *"Saying 'no' for someone else can be a dangerous thing and may keep you from establishing a strong relationship that could be helpful to everyone involved."*

- One large business headquarters that has such printing capabilities.

- One church with such printing capabilities.

- The small print shop at the local high school.

- The printing department at the local vocational school that offers high school and community college classes.

All these entities could probably fill your need for the 10,000 brochures. They have the presses, expertise, and skilled workers capable of doing so.

In looking at the publics file for each of these eight, you notice some crucial information on contacts and make up:

- You have no contact information in two of the three print shops in town.

- The third print shop is connected to your program through a volunteer who regularly uses their services. The person is an episodic, drop-in volunteer and you have not seen him in about three months.

- Two volunteers are married to spouses who work in the large company that could print the brochures for you. One is a secretary in the order department and the other is a salesman for the firm. The company is very involved in Habitat for Humanity and requires its workers to donate time to serve this charity.

- Several volunteers and staff members belong to the large church in town. Two are in leadership positions and one is related to the church secretary. The volunteers are very dedicated to your program and are involved in many of your activities.

- One staff person has a son in the print class at the high school. She knows they are busy right now doing all the programs, tickets, and posters for the prom which is two weeks away. Twelve

> *"Do your homework. Have someone research the giving and volunteering patterns of companies, organizations, and houses of faith in your area. Find and note the mission statements of such groups if possible. For those that match what you do, begin to cultivate key individuals within their ranks to explore collaboration opportunities."*

volunteers also have children at the high school. Two are very active on the board of the Parents Booster Club for the football team. Another happens to be a neighbor and good friend of the printing teacher. Another occasional volunteer is the guidance counselor at the school.

- Two volunteers have had children go through the print program at the local vocational high school and then go on to become printers out of state. One is a friend of the teacher. One student volunteer from the local high school is now enrolled by special permission in one of the more advanced classes held for college students every Thursday evening at the vocational high school. Through this student you learn that they have just completed an extensive project to print the campaign appeal of the YMCA, which is starting to raise funds to add to their facilities.

- You've been dealing with the newspaper for years and know the newest community affairs reporter fairly well (that position seems to turn over about every six months!). Almost all of your staff and volunteers are subscribers. The paper is always generous in featuring any news item you send them.

Keep in mind that the publics resource file gives you the names and contact information for those people already connected to you who have contacts to or within the publics that are of possible interest to you. These contacts could provide you additional information that is up to date and very specific.

Your next step is to prioritize your publics to see which might become markets to contact to fill your need as you fill a need of theirs (see the Prioritization Chart on page 37).

Again, brainstorm each public, listing the values you might offer each in return for printing the brochures. Begin to prioritize, looking for clues that eliminate or put any of the eight lower on the priority list of prospects. You are searching for your most likely success in getting what you need AND offering the most in return (the value for value exchange relationship).

> *" Prioritize your publics to see which might become markets to contact to fill your need as you fill a need of theirs. "*

Prioritization Chart

Need:	Potential Market:	Contact:	Value trade:
10,000 tri-fold, 3 color general informational brochures in 90 days	Vocational HS	Mark Jones, advanced student; 2 vols. had kids thru: now printers;	Experience; credit; students/program; example for resume one knows teacher of students; PR.
	Local HS print ed.	John Smith is Guidance Cnslr: 1 staff, 12 vols. have kids there. several are leaders among parents.	Student credit; good PR; example for resume.
	Church	Several vols. are members; some are leaders.	Good PR.
	Local business	2 vols. work there;	Good PR.
	The newspaper	Have direct contact; helpful in past	Community service; good PR.
	Printing Shop	Have a direct contact	Good PR. Very busy.

In this process you eliminate the two printing companies with which you have no contacts. They may be good to cultivate for the future, but your time is short and you are looking for more likely partners in this endeavor. You set aside the idea of approaching the newspaper because you already have to ask them for help several times a year to squeeze something in about your program or upcoming events.

You recognize that you have the most contacts at the high school and quite a few at the local vocational school. You have some contacts in the church and business and a thin contact with the third printing business. Looking just at contacts, your first priority looks like this:

1st choice: Local high school print shop program

2nd choice: Local vocational print program

3rd choice: The church

4th choice: The local business

5th choice: The newspaper

6th choice: The third print shop

As you consider the types of contacts you have within each of these groups and begin to list what you might trade in value to each, a clear "top priority" emerges. Your marketing plan is beginning to take shape.

As you look at this list, a few things should pop out: (1) that the two high schools offer you the most internal contacts, AND (2) that you have a lot of things to offer in return for their involvement. At this point your own good sense comes into play, because common knowledge tells you that there is one very big difference between the two programs:

- In the printing classes of the regular high school you have a mixture of motivations for the students enrolled. A few might be interested in making printing a career, but most are taking the course because they need an industrial arts credit to graduate!

- The vocational high school classes are for those younger students who have an interest in printing (as in the example of your student volunteer, Mark Jones). It also attracts adults of all ages who are taking the course through the community college. They have apparently made some decision about pursuing the trade of printing. The resume building, experience, and the good PR for the program itself take on greater weight, therefore, both for the students enrolled and those who might sign up in the future.

Given all the factors involved, the vocational print classes, which have just completed a major project and might be looking for another, become your number one target. Your number two priority is the high school, and so on down the line.

You never want to have just one targeted market. You want to have plan B, C, and D in mind in case you run into some new

> *You never want to have just one targeted market. You want to have plan B, C, and D in mind in case you run into some new information that makes it impossible for your top priority to work with you.*

information that makes it impossible for your top priority to work with you.

You have clearly identified who has what you need. Now you move on to determining how you might obtain the need (use Worksheet E on page 44 and Worksheet F on page 64).

Step 4. HOW do You GET What You Need?

When I first began training and was writing my book on marketing, I devised this four-step plan and, in my research, found that this fourth step of meeting marketing needs was more commonly referred to as a marketing strategy. Marketing experts went on and on, some in very complex terminology, to explain what strategizing entailed. My eyes often glazed over as they devoted page after page to this topic and that odd word: strategize. Even the dictionary devoted dozens of words to define the concept.

I found them all lacking in my basic principle of saying things directly and as simply as possible. "Never use quarter words when nickel ones will do," is a motto I teach and live by, so I decided to consult our son's junior high school dictionary which often followed this guiding rule of thumb. Sure enough, I found the definition that says it all as simply as possible:

> *Strategy: A clever way to make something happen.*

Yep, that's it—a clever way to get something done. It's another way to describe Step #4 in the marketing process: Figuring out how to get what you need. It even helped me re-state the four steps in simpler language:

> *What'cha got? What'cha need? Who's got it? How do ya get it?*

English teachers won't like that, but teaching audiences do because the colloquialisms get their attention and stick the con-

> *"Don't get discouraged if you do not successfully recruit or enlist any individual or organization on your first try. If you kept "friend-raising" in mind, consider it a win that you made a connection; expect involvement in the future."*

cepts on the front bulletin board of their minds! They simply don't forget the steps or their critical sequence.

As we continue to use the example of trying to get the 10,000 brochures, we go back to the information we have on the vocational high school and note that one of our current volunteers is very involved with the vocational program. He is taking a college level night class there and even a quick conversation with him tells you he is planning on making printing his career choice. He has made friends with the teacher, who is very pleased to have such a motivated young student.

You then recruit this student, Mark Jones, to help you approach the teacher. You find out when is the best time to approach him (after Thursday night class) and ask Mark to make a specific appointment.

You take along brochures from the past that have been done for you and a clear outline of what you need. You also take information to tell the teacher about your program and who is helped by your volunteers' efforts. You and Mark sit down with the teacher, take along a letter of reference from the other volunteers in your program who know him and, as agreed upon before the meeting, you and Mark outline verbally what you need, asking specifically for his help in having his students produce the brochure. You provide all the answers to the teacher's questions and note those that you cannot answer. Promise to get the information to him within 48 hours. You are brief, to the point, and open in your communication.

You outline your needs specifically and tell him what is in it for him and his students—benefits they might gain from involvement with this project.

You get a "yes" to your request and set up another meeting to go over timelines and plans for design and production. You agree that Mark will be the lead student on the project because he is an excellent printing student and knows the volunteer program personally.

> " *Train everyone around you to think of themselves as constant marketers. The need to speak on your program's behalf, enlisting new support, telling stories of people served.* "

In this final step, you have integrated the art of asking, human motivation, and the offer of a solid exchange relationship. You have been direct and forthright and have the beginning of a healthy trade of value for value. You have not left without getting a specific commitment and setting up the next contacts and a procedure for communication.

It's a good match and you will get what you need.

Inherent in this example are the critical principles of meeting your need by asking the right person for the right thing at the right time and place and by offering what is valued and appreciated by them. Often the marketing process falls on its face when the wrong person is asked for inappropriate objects at the wrong time. My art-teacher husband always warned friends that the first week of his junior high classes was so hectic that it was the wrong time to ask for any special favors. Be careful to strategize carefully and with good counsel so that the timing, target, request, and exchange are positioned correctly (see Worksheet G on page 65).

> *"In this final step, you have integrated the art of asking, human motivation, and the offer of a solid exchange relationship."*

WORKSHEET C
(to be used with large and diverse groups in your community)
CURRENT PUBLIC PERCEPTION: AN AUDIT

Thank you for agreeing to complete this survey. It will help us learn how much our community knows about what we do.

Name of your organization:_____   Today's date:_____

Information about you personally: ☐ Male   ☐ Female

Age: ☐ Under 15   ☐ 22-35   ☐ 46-55   ☐ 66-75   ☐ 76-85   ☐ Over 85
      ☐ Married   ☐ Single   ☐ Own home   ☐ Rent   ☐ Other:_____
      ☐ In school   ☐ Work full time   ☐ Work part time   ☐ Not working*   ☐ Retired
      *outside of home

1. Describe what you know about our organization:

2. Have you heard of us?   ☐ Yes   ☐ No   ☐ Not sure

3. Which of the following areas do we serve? (check as many as apply)
   ☐ Arts   ☐ Children   ☐ Human Services   ☐ Shelter   ☐ Crisis   ☐ Elderly
   ☐ Environment   ☐ Hunger   ☐ Homeless   ☐ Safety   ☐ Beautification
   ☐ Health   ☐ Education   ☐ Other?_____

4. What efforts do we sponsor in the community?

5. What is our reputation?   ☐ Excellent   ☐ Good   ☐ Fair   ☐ Poor   ☐ Don't know
   To what do you attribute this reputation?

6. How effective do you believe we are in utilizing volunteers?
   ☐ Excellent   ☐ Good   ☐ Fair   ☐ Poor   ☐ Don't know
To what do you attribute this reputation?

Would you be interested in becoming a volunteer for us?   ☐ Yes   ☐ No   ☐ Not sure
(If you would like more information on what we do or how you might become involved, please tear off the bottom portion and hand it in with this survey.)

- -

Date:_____

Name:_____   Phone #:_____

Address:_____   City:_____

State:_____   Zip:_____

I would like: ☐ More information   ☐ To be on your mailing list   ☐ To volunteer

WORKSHEET D
OUR ORGANIZATION OR PROGRAM POSITION*

Name of Program:

Mission Statement:**

What we do: (events, services, programs, products, tasks, etc.)

Who is our competition and what makes us distinctive from each competitor?

What does the public THINK we do?***

What do we WANT the public to know about us?

Who might help us get our message across?

How might we get this message across?

What do we want our position in the community to be one year from now? (position goal)

What first steps might we take toward this goal?

What competition will we have for this position? Can we collaborate with any competition?

*Can be used to determine community or internal organizational position.
**If you don't have one, STOP! and create one. Without this roadmap, you won't know where you're going.
***From Public Perception provided in this booklet.

Worksheet E
Future Planning for Public Perception

1. What is the current public perception of

   a. Your organization:

   b. The volunteer program:

2. What are the strongest points of these perceptions?

3. What are the weakest points of these perceptions?

4. How might you erase negative images in the perceptions?

5. What do you want the general public to think about your volunteer program two years from now? (Your goal)

6. What steps might you plan today to help you achieve this positive perception goal?

Chapter 3

The Art of Asking

Intertwined in the marketing process is the ability of the marketer (recruiter) to ask for and receive specific support. As critical as it is to understand the principles and process of marketing, it is equally important to master the art of asking.

Typically people make requests of others in the hope that they will get a "yes" response. I would suggest that in marketing our volunteer programs, there is a different approach that is more effective:

Instead of trying to get people to say "yes," you should work to remove their reasons to say "no."

The difference between the two approaches is subtle, yet appropriate for the kinds of things we typically ask of others. In recruitment, for example, removing reasons to say "no" eliminates any arm-twisting, pleas by guilt, deceptive promotion, and other methods that mask the asker's overriding need to fill an open job slot rather than a desire to match people and assignments in a fair trade of value for everyone.

As demands on people's time and energy increase, it is important to predict why people might say "no" and then plan asking strategies to eliminate or reduce these "no" responses. A word of caution, however: Never fraudulently remove a "no." In other words, don't lie about a negative in the hope that recruits won't back out when they find out they were misled! They may go ahead and complete the assignment, but their trust will have been destroyed and chances are they will not work for you again AND (worse yet) they will tell others about the deception. This is a de-marketing result.

> *"Instead of trying to get people to say 'yes,' you should work to remove their reasons to say 'no.'"*

> *Never fraudulently remove a 'no.' In other words, don't lie about a negative in the hope that recruits won't back out when they find out they were misled!*

When working with staff in an organization and trying to persuade them to accept assistance that volunteers might bring to their work, keep the "no-removal concept" in mind. Often staff are resistant to having to supervise volunteers because of previous bad experiences or fears that are unfounded. Try to anticipate these fears, ask other staff members to share their positive experiences with their colleague as an example, and remove their "nos."

Hidden Questions

There are questions people have in their mind whenever anyone is asking something of them. They are especially powerful in the minds of potential volunteers as we are asking for their two most precious resources: time and energy. Understand these hidden questions and be prepared to answer them BEFORE the prospect even asks them. Do not be misled if they do not verbalize the questions.

The hidden questions:

1. What do you want from me? (to do, give, share, or support)

2. What amounts will you need from me? (time, energy, money, resources, or goods)

3. What is in it for me? (satisfaction, value, needs, or wants)

4. Why should I trust you? (track record, reputation, reliability, or process)

> *Understand hidden questions and be prepared to answer them BEFORE the prospect even asks them.*

Potential supporters may have very specific questions for you that fall outside of the four listed above. It will be up to you to think of these in advance and have answers ready. For example, to recruit people to work in a health care setting, you can anticipate questions on safety; to recruit people to work in a museum, you can anticipate questions on extensive training on artifacts.

ASKING TECHNIQUES

There are four categories of asking:

1. Asking in person, one on one.

2. Asking a group.

3. Asking over the phone or electronically, via e-mail.

4. Asking in writing, including fax.

Please understand that all four asking techniques can be weighted for or against success, depending on interpersonal relationships. Thus, if in any of the above techniques the person ASKING is known personally by the person receiving the request, there is more likelihood of success. Also, if the person being asked knows of the asker, even though they may not know each other personally, the chance of a positive response is more likely. When the people being asked do NOT know the asker, either directly or by reputation, the chances of a positive response decline.

Also, understand that there can be weight added to appeals simply because of the reputation of the organization. Americans respond quite favorably to appeals from groups such as the American Red Cross and Salvation Army because they trust the organizations and can see how they serve people. This is true of pleas to support child services and animal rescue.

Let's look at the asking techniques in greater depth:

1. Asking in Person

Asking in person is by far the most effective method, even though it takes the most time. When you don't directly know the prospect, it is wise to take an "authenticator" with you when you make your

> *"Regardless of technique, if the person asking is known personally by the person receiving the request, there is more likelihood of success."*

An organization is more likely to get a positive response if the person being asked knows of the asker—even if there is no personal acquaintance.

This factor tells you why so many direct mail marketing companies try to get a well-known celebrity figure to be the voice of the asker.

> *Friend-raising is successful even if the prospects being asked say "no" to specific appeals.*

Advantages

The one-to-one, in-person approach has many advantages over the other asking techniques:

- It lends urgency to the appeal.

- It can establish a personal relationship.

- It can provide immediate response to questions posed by the prospect.

- It lends credibility to the cause and appeal.

- It produces more and larger results.

- It offers opportunities to remove reasons to say "no."

continued

appeal, so that they can vouch for your credibility, the proposed project, or other forms of involvement.

Remember our example of the printing of 10,000 brochures? The approach used included the volunteer director taking Mark, a printing student, along when appealing to Mark's teacher. Mark was the "authenticator"; his very presence said, "I know this volunteer manager and trust her; you can too."

The in-person approach is used when stakes are high. You are looking for lead donors in a capital campaign; a lead volunteer in a major event; a high official in your own organization who must give permission for a new effort or change you are proposing; a critical door-opener in the community who must be for, rather than against, you if you are to bring a new effort to your area successfully.

The Art of FRIEND-Raising.

Friend-raising is a descriptive phrase that helps people grasp the wider scope of resource attainment, which includes recruitment and support as well as the more popular phrase of fund raising. It also expands the concept of asking, because if friend-raising is the goal, there can be few "failures."

Friend-raising is successful even if the prospects being asked say "no" to specific appeals. You can simply ask to keep them informed of the program's efforts. If they say "yes" to this (as most do), you still have a thread of connection that can prove beneficial in the future. Even if the person never works directly with your program, if they remain informed and tell others about your work, you may turn them into an agent that speaks in your behalf! If they say "no" to the request to keep in touch, they will respect your adhering to their preference, and at the very least may not put any roadblocks in your path as you pursue your effort.

In regard to the person who prefers not to be kept informed, do not minimize the importance of discovering people with very negative feelings about what you are doing. Knowing who your roadblocks might be is as important as knowing who your strongest supporters are! Forewarned is forearmed.

In the following segment, please take note of the guidelines for asking a group because they are the same as when you are asking an individual.

2. Asking A Group

The second best method of asking is to make your request in person to a group of people. Typically this occurs when a person makes a presentation to a membership group, a board of directors, or a small body of decision-makers. In presenting such an appeal, keep the following things in mind:

Do your homework.

Know as much about your audience as possible. If it is a membership group, try to find a member already connected to you who can tell you about the group's structure, calendar, reward system, governance, history, goals, past support of your organization, giving and involvement patterns, leaders, and founders. It is assumed you already have a lot of this information in your resource file.

State your case simply.

The fewer carefully chosen words you use, the more effective you will be. Who are you? What is your organization about? Whom do you propose to help? What do you want the group to do? How legitimate is your cause? Do your homework before proposing your effort. What competition do you have? If it is a new effort, what measures do you have in place to make it successful? Why is it important?

- It establishes direct, clean communication.

- It can diagnose any objections the prospect might have.

- It can diagnose and erase any misinformation or even disinformation.

- It can redirect support if the person is reluctant to say yes to a specific request, but is obviously interested in helping in some other area of your program.

- It adds information to your resource file; you can pick up pertinent information that can be used at a later time.

- It allows the asker to accept a "no" for the present, but stay in touch for future involvement.

All of the above and many of the other techniques in asking are critical for long-term success.

Ask for and respond directly and honestly to questions.

If you don't know the answer to any questions, don't fake it! Tell them you will get the answer to them in 48 hours or less. Be forthright.

Vary your presentation; mix visuals with verbal appeals.

Understand that there are different types of learners. Some take in information and process it by hearing it; others process information by reading about it, and still others learn by experiencing new information either physically or emotionally. The group in-person approach obviously satisfies those people who learn through hearing you present your case verbally. Those who learn by reading will absorb your message more thoroughly by having something in writing: a general brochure, endorsements, history, or a chart of financial matters. The experiential learner can be more difficult to inform. I suggest you use some actual stories of clients served to help them "feel" the importance of your work. Using visuals such as videos and slides can help in this regard. A previous client telling his or her story can be most effective as long as it does not overdo sentimentality or lean toward a guilt appeal.

Use the language of the audience.

Know what terms might appeal to them. Know their own internal routes to rewards. If they are part of a larger organization, know how they earn respect from that parent group. If a corporation honors those divisions which provide the most innovative community service, make your appeal with that goal in mind. If a youth group gets badges for service, include that prospect in your appeal. Tailor your language to the interests of the group as they dovetail with your mission or plans. As long as you are being honest and not trying to "con" a group by misleading them, this tailoring is simply a respect for their interest and a way to bring about a successful collaboration.

> *" A previous client telling his or her story can be most effective as long as it does not overdo sentimentality or lean toward a guilt appeal. "*

Share your own commitment.

Often the demonstration of your own commitment and telling why you became involved helps people understand how important the cause can become to an individual. Stress your own belief that you are making a difference. A basic motivation for many people, as they decide how and where they will spend their time and energy, is the impact of the work.

Ask in terms of clients served, not the organization.

People want to help people; they are not as interested in helping institutions. As our world becomes more and more automated, distanced, and mechanical, we long for human contact. Help your audience see the real people they can serve—clients, students, and the general public—through their involvement.

Have help.

Take along others who can help you spot and talk to people in the audience who seem the most interested, have questions, or are obviously the ones the rest of the group looks to for leadership. If you have people already working with your program who are also members of the group before you, they are usually the best persuaders to have with you.

Get the names and contact information for those most interested or those who are obviously "door openers" for you.

Don't leave without getting specific information about key folks who have heard your message. If follow-up appeals are necessary or further action required, you want to be able to deal directly with individuals.

Requests "in person" to a group can be very effective if done properly and recognized as just a first step in establishing a relationship

> *Help your audience see the real people they can serve—clients, students, and the general public—through their involvement.*

> *The trick is to identify quickly those key individuals who can help you advance your goal of an equitable trade of value for value.*

Rules to Govern Phone or E-mail Appeals

- Have your critical points in writing and in front of you before the contact.

- Be brief, clear, and to the point.

- Listen for opportunities to answer questions and build rapport. Ask for questions and promise a quick response.

- Be courteous. Do not take any "no" personally. Do not respond in anger should the contacted person become angry.

- Relay any questions you can't answer to those who can respond quickly.

- If the people state that they do not wish to have another contact, record and transmit this information to the people who can remove them from a calling list.

---

in which both entities can benefit. The trick is to identify quickly those key individuals who can help you advance your goal of an equitable trade of value for value.

3. Asking by Phone or E-mail

Requests by phone or by e-mail are less likely to get a positive response because it is easier for people to say "no" when they are not having to look someone in the eye. E-mail can be even more impersonal, as the prospect does not even have to hear the asker's voice. There are times, however, when phone solicitation is necessary, and even when it can be effective because the person called knows either the caller or the cause.

Christian churches typically recruit teachers for their Sunday schools via the phone; membership groups are using e-mail more and more to ask members to participate in a specific community project, and corporations often spread the word about the need for volunteers on a particular project via voice or e-mail.

One community service award-winning company has a 24 hour volunteer service hot line that continually updates workers as to service needs, telling them where to get more specific information on job assignments, timing and signing up. It works!

Again, you can see that the impact these appeals have depends on the relationship between the asker, the cause, and the prospects. When there is no relationship, the request is most likely to fail; when there is one, it will be more successful.

Understand that such appeals are often more scatter-gun and non-specific than targeted, and expectations of return are predictably less than the in-person techniques.

Unless the person called is familiar with your program or you, this method can take a lot of time and lead to a great deal of frustration. It is better to train 20 people to make ten "in-person" appeals each than to have five people sit and call those same 200. It will get more positive results.

4. Asking in Writing: Letters or Fax

Appeals in writing are the least likely to get a positive response, especially if there is no prior relationship between the prospect and the person or cause sending the communiqué. Understand that you are dealing with direct mail, and in the marketing industry, a return rate of only 1-3% can be expected from a shotgun (nonspecific), direct mail appeal of this nature. The real goal is to cull out the 1-3% who do respond and go to them over and over again!

The rules of clarity and brevity apply more to the written appeal than any other.

You must state your case clearly, define WHO is to be helped through the prospect's involvement and ask specifically for a commitment.

These marketing appeals need to be as personalized and relational as possible. The need for continual marketing through the media to tell the story of what you do, what you need, and who you would like to engage becomes painfully clear in the wake of a dismal response to a direct mail campaign because the community simply didn't recognize the organization sending the appeal. It has happened over and over again, and I am always bemused by the shock on the faces of the organization hierarchy who believed that, "Everyone surely knows who we are!"

Public Perception

Incorrect assumptions about your public image and recognition can be deadly when you are trying to build support for volunteers, donations, or assistance. To test the public awareness of your organization or program, enlist the help of several civic groups, churches, or temples, asking for permission to survey their members. In the

---

Examples of Survey Questions

1. We are the Junior Women's Club of Downers Grove. Have you ever heard of us?

2. What do we do?

3. What kind of a group are we:
   Open membership?
   Invitational?
   Other:_____

4. What projects have you heard associated with our name?

5. What is your general opinion of us? (Worksheet C on page 42 is a sample assessment.)

For a volunteer program in an organization or facility, your questionnaire might offer:

1. We are the volunteer program at Good Samaritan Hospital. Have you heard of us?

continued

2. Who can belong to this program? Who now belongs?

3. What do you think we do?

4. How does one become involved with us?

5. Do you believe there are any restrictions or demands on our volunteers? If so, what are they?

* Misinformation is incorrect information given out or passed along by those who believe it to be true. It inadvertently does damage.

** Dis-information is incorrect information given out or passed along by those who know it to be false. When negative, it is intended to do damage or "under cut" someone or something. It can be deadly. Knowing it exists, however, is you best defense as you begin to erase it.

survey, ask questions without signaling the answers you want to hear. See the questions in the sidebar for examples.

Do not take the above questions as gospel for your particular situation. Create your own survey to measure what is important for you to know in uncovering the public perception and depth of understanding of what you are about. If the survey responses reveal a good grasp of what you do and who you are, you can proceed with public contacts. If, however, they reveal misinformation* or even dis-information**, you will need to design a marketing campaign to provide the public with more accurate information. This is a critical base for any type of marketing you might plan for the future.

MOTIVATION AND ASKING

We do not need to get Ph.D.s in motivational theory to help us understand why some appeals are more warmly received than others. David McClelland's Motivational Theory is a good basic source for understanding why some appeals are more successful than others.

The critical teaching of his work is that each of us prefers some approaches over others, depending on what turns us "on" or "off." McClelland's research divides human motivations into three categories, although you need to understand that we all have all three at some level of our being. It is just that one typically dominates the other two. The three classifications are:

People motivated by RELATIONSHIPS

These folks prefer people-contact work. They like to work in teams or committees, avoid isolation, be liked, and have good relationships with others. They prefer approaches that include the asker's own motivations and stories about the clients who can be helped if they simply volunteer. They typically ask for assignments that provide direct contact with others. They define success in terms of people and how they feel while being served or serving.

People motivated by ACHIEVEMENT

These folks want work that allows them to quantify their efforts; they respond to facts, data and numbers. They like people, but work well alone with specific direction. They want supervisors to monitor their progress so that they know they are heading in the right direction. They define success in terms of numbers and accountable advancements. They love to excel, to race against others, and, of course, to win. Bigger is better; more is master. How many people are served or serving is important to them.

*People motivated by EMPOWERMENT****

They want work that allows them to impact and influence others or situations. These people feel challenged when someone tells them something can't be done. They want a free rein and do not feel the need to be loved or monitored by supervisors. Just tell them what needs to be accomplished and let them do it! They can work alone or in groups, but can be overbearing in their drive to change situations. They think in terms of long-range visions. How people or situations will be different in the future is important to them. Quality of life is often their goal; they typically gravitate to jobs that allow them to persuade, effect change, influence, educate, or inform.

I have changed McClelland's term to "EM-powerment" to signal a more positive definition.

As you examine these classifications, some light bulbs may be going on in your head! You may have the answer to why the high-powered influencer did not respond to the opportunity to be on the social committee for the hospital volunteer ball, or why the volunteer who loved to hug everyone and make newcomers feel so comfortable rejected the idea of transcribing old meeting notes at a

> *"When marketing any type of idea or appeal, the more you know about people's motivation or what turns them on, the better your chance will be to involve them."*

***   McClelland used the word "Power" for this third classification.

home computer. They were looking for work more in line with their motivations.

When marketing any type of idea or appeal, the more you know about people's motivation or what turns them on, the better your chance will be to involve them. When you need some support for a major change in your own organization, it is critical to know how to approach and enlist key leaders who can help influence decision making.

When attempting to enlist new leadership-level volunteers, your best results will come when you have a job that matches their dominant motivation. Thus, the volunteer who loves to make people feel welcome and is a "class-A hugger" will probably respond positively to an assignment on the welcoming and orientation committee for new volunteers.

Understanding motivation and matching people to jobs accordingly is yet another way for us to demonstrate our caring concern for the volunteers who can provide what we need. Placing the right people in the right jobs is a rather inconspicuous, but golden, gift we can give to others in return for their support.

> *Placing the right people in the right jobs is a rather inconspicuous, but golden, gift we can give to others in return for their support.*

DIAGNOSING OBJECTIONS

In the asking process, we will encounter people who express reluctance to become involved. Because our goal is to remove "no(s)" rather than arm-twist to pull a "yes" from them, it is critical to understand what is at the root of their reluctance.

Why people say no:

- They are committed to another project.

- Involvement would be in conflict with a value they hold (abortion rights, for example).

- They have a life circumstance (illness, impending move) that would prevent involvement at this time.

- They feel they are already overloaded with tasks.

- They recognize they are not really interested in what you are proposing.

These are not truly objections, but simply realities that would stand in the way of their becoming involved.

Others have true objections, however, and it is important for you to get to the source of these objections and remove those that you honestly can. I insert the word "honestly" because I have run across those people who will promise anything to get someone to support their effort. I cannot think of a worse way start a relationship or a more sure-fire way to destroy credibility and trust than being less than truthful during a marketing appeal. Besides being deceptive, it suggests that the asker does not consider the prospect bright enough to figure out the hoax, thereby adding insult to injury!

As you listen to people respond to your asking appeals and hear them moving toward a "no" response, try to diagnose what their objections are. Here are some clues that might guide you in your diagnosis:

There are seven common objections. They are listed here along with suggestions on how to remove them.

1. The Stall

The prospect tries to postpone action and avoid commitment. Often this is a mask indicating uncertainty of what they need to do to be successful. Respond by being very clear about their duties, what help they will receive, and the importance of making a decision quickly to help the clients to be served (remember, people work for people, not entities).

Have you answered all the hidden questions?

- What do you want?

- What will it cost?

- What's the return value to me?

- How much time will it take?

- Can I trust you?

2. The Big "D"—Doubt

This typically signals a lack of confidence in either you or your program/organization. Offer proof of any claims you make and the trustworthiness of your organization. Provide audits, history, leaders' names, and peers to contact for personal references.

3. Requests for Reassurance

In our exceedingly impersonal world where PIN numbers have replaced our name, people want to be reassured that they are considered to be valuable individuals and that you will not lead them into failure.

Offer honest feedback on how they will be supported and that you and your program care about their success because you care about them as people. They will typically not be willing to voice the fact that they need personal reassurance of your support.

4. Coax Me

Some folks simply want to be coaxed. It's a game with them. They offer resistance to see how hard you are willing to work to get them to sign on. Sometimes that comes from a need to feel more valuable; sometimes it is because they have a hard time making a decision and need a bit more time to think about the request. You can use gentle, positive pressure in response, laying out what the trade of value for value will be for each of you, but be careful. Arm-twisting a reluctant prospect can cause you untold grief in the long run by placing a very "right" person in a "wrong" or non-match job!

5. Hidden Agenda

This is the most challenging and difficult objection to diagnose and respond to, as it is so murky in nature. As you present your request,

> *In our exceedingly impersonal world where PIN numbers have replaced our name, people want to be reassured that they are considered to be valuable individuals.*

> *Some folks simply want to be coaxed. They offer resistance to see how hard you are willing to work to get them to sign on.*

you note that the prospect keeps giving you different responses, which seem like excuses for non-commitment. When you try to remove objections they give you a new excuse. All of these "no"s signal some hidden agenda. Their responses often seem illogical and contrived. All you can do is to try to get to the bottom of their thinking and respond accordingly.

Keep in mind that a hidden agenda may be no more devious than the fact that they simply don't want to accept your proposal and don't want to hurt your feelings by a direct "no." Never talk anyone with a hidden agenda into working with you. Keep in mind that sometimes the response that is truly in the best interests of everyone concerned is a "no."

" Keep in mind that sometimes the response that is truly in the best interests of everyone concerned is a 'no.' "

6. Mistaken Objections

Occasionally a prospect has wrong information about you, your clients, or organization. A group I once worked with provided volunteers for a prison-support program. They realized that their poor recruitment responses were stemming from a public assumption that all volunteers who worked with them would be asked to go to the prison to work directly with inmates. That was not the case. Those direct-service volunteer assignments that did require a trip to the prison and inmate contact had safety factors in place to reassure the most timid recruit.

The organization reversed their poor recruitment response rate by putting stories in the local paper about the variety of jobs open to volunteers, having current volunteers offer presentations, presenting slides, giving accurate information to groups and churches, and beginning all recruiting appointments with a clarification of the location and type of work to carried out.

Root out mistaken objections. Identify them as misinformation or dis-information and work to offer the correct information.

7. Hard Objections

On occasion you will encounter those individuals or groups who have requests that you cannot meet. They demand a value return to them that is not possible, such as stating that they will only volunteer for you if you will support an effort of theirs that is not part of your mission or authority. Another example is having a prospect tell you that they cannot give you a commitment unless you drop an effort with which they do not agree. Such objections typically mean that you will have to settle for simply making a friend rather than getting a "yes" to your request.

Through all of these objections and the wider topic of asking, one rule dominates over everything else: Never promise what you can't deliver!

Honesty, integrity, and trust are the most important "products" you will ever market. Never do anything to jeopardize or tarnish any of them. It is better to get a "no" and make a friend than to get a "yes" through less-than-honest and -forthright promises.

> *Honesty, integrity, and trust are the most important 'products' you will ever market.*

PROMOTIONAL OPTIONS

Before we leave the topic of Asking, it is important to understand the variety of promotional options that are open to us. Whether we are targeting the general public in an attempt to recruit volunteers or are simply (but often with more difficulty) trying to get peers or the hierarchy in our organization to appreciate and offer greater support to the volunteer program, we are having to use promotional techniques to persuade.

There are four options open to us in promoting our cause:

1.   Advertising

2.   Publicity

3. Promotion

4. Personal Selling

Advertising

Advertising is a campaign that is designed, pre-tested on a target market, post-tested to measure results, and presented through selected media avenues. Ads usually have a slogan or theme geared to specific audiences to attain maximum commitments. They are usually paid for, although some may be placed in newspapers, being "piggybacked" with ads local merchants offer. Such advertisers are therefore donating some of their space to the cause, a clever way for you to get ads out to the public without having to pay for them directly.

The biggest mistake made in advertising is that nonprofit leaders who are inexperienced in marketing assume they can simply drop an ad in any newspaper and sit back to wait for the responses. This usually does not happen, as such an ad has not been tested or really targeted. It's a shotgun approach and might serve as one way to get name recognition, but little else.

An ad, however, placed in a retirement community's newsletter and written to appeal to people over the age of 55 who have disposable time and a desire to be involved in a effort that could effect them directly will probably bring great results. It can be easily tested before full release on a similar community and post-tested for results. It meets the requirements for good advertisements.

Publicity

Publicity is the effort a program makes to get its message and news about what it is doing out to the public. It is designed "to bring favorable attention to a product, person, organization, place, or cause" according to Theodore Levitt, the author of *The Marketing Imagination*.

> *"The biggest mistake made in advertising is that nonprofit leaders who are inexperienced in marketing assume they can simply drop an ad in any newspaper and sit back to wait for the responses."*

It differs from advertising because it is typically carried by the media at no cost and without reference to who wrote it.

Promotion

Promotion is defined as marketing activities other than personal selling; that is, ads or publicity that help get a message out to the public. Often I hear about volunteer programs that participate in an Information Fair at a local shopping mall, whereby each community organization has a booth on a given day that informs shoppers about activities and opportunities for involvement. That is a promotion.

Volunteer Centers across North America can typically be the driving force behind such fairs and invite volunteer program and community service groups to participate. They can also be the source of other ways to promote a cause, making them an invaluable ally in any marketing efforts.

Personal Selling

Personal Selling brings us full-circle in looking at the "art of asking." Being able to look someone in the eye when you are describing your need and the ways in which they might become involved will always be the most effective.

The times in which we live demand that we are constantly having to sing the praises of our volunteer programs. For years this has been an external effort, as we marketed needs to the community in recruitment, fund raising, and resource development efforts.

Today, however, we often find that the biggest marketing challenges can be internal as we must keep colleagues, peers, and the hierarchy in our corner so that when decisions are made as to allocations of money and support, the volunteer department is not left out or put at the bottom of a priority list.

> *"Being able to look someone in the eye when you are describing your need and the ways in which they might become involved will always be the most effective."*

The volunteer managers of the 21st century need to be constant advocates and marketers of their programs. They make sure people who make decisions about the life and health of the department are continually made aware of the importance of volunteers to the organization.

The roles of volunteer managers have changed dramatically in the last decade and include a need to be internal consultants and power brokers. They must make sure that everyone who needs to understand the value of the volunteer program does so and is willing to stand up and be counted when the chips are down.

This role demands an understanding and facility with the concepts and "how-to's" of marketing, making sure that the caring trade of value for value includes basic survival of the program and allocation of resources to keep it viable.

Knowing how to leverage information, use clout effectively, demonstrate specific benefits of having volunteers involved, and use power to empower is critical not only to success in the 21st century, but surviving and thriving!

It's not easy, but it's worth it.

> *The roles of volunteer managers have changed dramatically in the last decade and include a need to be internal consultants and power brokers.*

Worksheet F
Marketing Planning Chart

Need*	Who has?**	What offer in return?	Key leaders:	Your contacts:	Notes

*Be specific: numbers, dates needed, etc.
**Rank by priority.

WORKSHEET G
MARKETING'S EIGHT KEY QUESTIONS

Use this format as you plan marketing strategies for efforts.

1. What does your program (event/effort/product) offer?

2. Who are the potential target markets which might be interested in your offering?

3. What are the needs and interests of those potential markets?

4. Which of these needs/interests can your offering provide?

5. How will you tell your target markets about your offering?

6. Who can help you reach and persuade each target market?

7. Prioritize your approaches: Set your best shot at #1; your second best shot at #2, and so on.

8. What are the first steps you will take to establish an exchange relationship?

Bibliography

Independent Sector. *Giving and Volunteering in the United States.* Washington, DC, 1996.

Kotler, Philip. *Marketing for Nonprofit Organizations.* Englewood, NJ: Prentice-Hall, 1975.

Levinson, Jay Conrad. *Guerrilla Marketing for the 90's.* Boston: Houghton-Mifflin Co., 1993.

Levitt, Theodore. *The Marketing Imagination.* New York: The Free Press, 1983.

Macduff, Nancy. *Volunteer Recruiting and Retention: A Marketing Approach.* Walla Walla, WA: MBA Publishing, 1996.

McCurley, Steve & Rick Lynch. *Volunteer Management: Mobilizing All The Resources of the Community.* Downers Grove, IL*: Heritage Arts Publishing.

McCurley, Steve. *Recruiting Volunteers for Difficult & Long Term Assignments.* Downers Grove, IL: Heritage Arts, 1991.

Montana, Patrick. *Marketing in Nonprofit Organizations.* New York: Amacom, 1978.

Popcorn, Faith. *The Popcorn Report.* New York: Doubleday, 1990-1997 (on-going).

Schoomaker, Alan Ph.D. *Selling: The Psychological Approach.* Control Data Corporation, 1978.

Shapiro, Benson P. *Marketing for Nonprofit Organizations.* Harvard Business Review, 1973.

Stern, Gary. *Marketing Workbook for Nonprofit Organizations.* St. Paul, NM: Wilder Foundation, 1997.

Vineyard, Sue. *Beyond Banquets, Plaques & Pins: Creative Ways to Recognize Volunteers.* Downers Grove, IL: Heritage Arts, 1999.

Vineyard, Sue. *Marketing Magic for Volunteer Programs*.* Downers Grove, IL: Heritage Arts, 1984.

Vineyard, Sue. *Megatrends & Volunteerism: Mapping the Future for Volunteer Programs.* Downers Grove, IL: Heritage Arts, 1993.

These books and reports can assist you in learning more about critical aspects of marketing for nonprofit organizations and programs.

* out of print

Vineyard, Sue. *Secrets of Motivation: How to GET and KEEP Volunteers & Paid Staff!* Downers Grove, IL: Heritage Arts Publishing, 1991.

Tips and Tricks for Marketing Magic!

1. Get to know key people in all media outlets; establish a good rapport.

2. Start small; work up to larger efforts.

3. Keep it as simple as possible.

4. Train everyone around you to think of themselves as constant marketers. The need to speak on your program's behalf, enlisting new support, telling stories of people served.

5. When orienting new volunteers, ask them to think of themselves as part of a dedicated "recruitment team," always on the lookout for new recruits. You might even supply them with calling cards to give to people who seem interested. The cards would have the name and number of the person to contact for involvement as well as your program's mission and location.

6. Get companies to design and print your brochures and newsletters.

7. Get advertisers to devote a small share of their newspaper ads to promote your program.

8. Create several speakers bureaus to give talks to groups and organizations.

9. Buy a gross of greeting cards and send them to key people, such as media contacts, just to keep the lines of contact open

A big thank you to Mike King, marketer-extraordinaire, with whom I have trained audiences in the art of marketing and who kindly offers many of these tips to help people make marketing work for them.

between you. Halloween and Valentines Day are great times to say "hi."

10. Read trends information to spot shifts that could reshape your marketing appeals.

11. Piggyback on anything that can bring more name recognition to your program.

12. If you want to launch a major marketing effort, create a task force of professionals in public relations, advertising, or media to help advise you in your planning.

13. As you accomplish goals, send a note to board members and internal hierarchy thanking them for their support in launching the effort. Constantly remind these folks of how important volunteers are to the organization.

14. Find creative ways to recognize and thank volunteers for all they do; don't forget to continually "market" your program to those already involved. This pays off in terms of staying-power and what they tell others about you.

15. To avoid de-marketing, ask everyone to follow this simple instruction: "If you like it, tell others; if you don't, tell me."

16. Utilize "adoption" to cement a relationship between a business, for example, and your program.

17. Have logo slicks, news releases, and drop-in ads ready for every possible use.

18. Piggyback on the efforts of others. If the bank will allow it, ask that every person going through the drive-through windows be given a promotion flier for your project. Ask utility companies to offer an insert in their bills or a note printed directly on their invoice. Ask grocery stores to tuck a flier in all sacks.

> *" Don't forget to continually 'market' your program to those already involved. "*

19. Remember that the most carefully read information pieces are newsletters. People read them because they know there can be news there that impacts them directly. Find out who the newsletter editors are of every major organization, business and house of faith and cultivate them as agent publics who can relay promotional information to their circle of acquaintances.

20. Make certain that everyone who is to go out in public and speak for your organization is very well trained. Give them more information than they can possibly use!

21. Do not assume that everyone can be a public speaker. Try them out first.

22. Create a consistent look in your written materials using color, design, and typeface.

23. Create an easy-to-remember, one-sentence description of what you do and then have everyone memorize it for use with folks just finding out about you.

24. If your organization name does not describe what you do (e.g., *The Isaak Walton League**), add a tag line that tells your purpose.

25. Don't assume everyone knows how to get in touch with you; check the yellow pages and community directory for ease of locating you.

26. Hand deliver prepared press releases.

27. Do your homework. Have someone research the giving and volunteering patterns of companies, organizations, and houses of faith in your area. Find and note the mission statements of such groups if possible. For those that match what you do, begin to cultivate key individuals within their ranks to explore collaboration opportunities.

> *"Keep in mind that everything you do is marketing. Everything."*

* an environmental association

28. Don't get discouraged if you do not successfully recruit or enlist any individual or organization on your first try. If you kept "friend-raising" in mind, consider it a win that you made a connection; expect involvement in the future.

29. Never assume anything. It will get you in trouble every time.

30. Keep in mind that everything you do is marketing. Everything.